The Holyoke Diaries

Gerald Yelle

FUTURECYCLE PRESS

www.futurecycle.org

*Cover art, "City Hall, Holyoke, Massachusetts, USA" by Joe Mabel;
floral background by Kevin Tuck (rgbstock.com); cover and interior book
design by Diane Kistner (dkistner@futurecycle.org); Calisto MT text
with Fertigo Pro titling*

Published by FutureCycle Press
Lexington, Kentucky, USA

ISBN 978-1-938853-53-1

For Jenny

Contents

Alley Culture

The ragman's visits kick up summer's lull, spinning waves
of haze and wheels, the clop and clang
of hooves and chains, the sing-song call for irreparables
—cloth he'll sell to a paper mill.

Five-year-old Monica pats the horse's flanks and nestles
up to its muzzle. She doesn't make it flinch the way flies do.

Part dust and dog-day bustle, part pageant hung mid-air:
garbage tossed on a conveyor belt or shoveled from chutes
—up three steps to dieseling dump trucks.

Two-year-old Mossy sleeps on walls and falls three feet.
Sleeps on the way to the hospital. Four-year-old Jim
has a patch on his eye. His brother Porky's three and falls
four flights. He'll live to have trouble with school.

The clothesline pole's a "ghoul" and goal. The hill's
for hiding in burdock, sumac, sapling and yew. The rusted
fence leads to drops from Jesso's soda-machine empties.

Broken branches are rifles for combat. The incinerator
near the end of the alley: a pillbox, ringed with raked bits
of glass, bees, ash and the smell of it. I lead my platoon warily.

Kids use torn sheets and cardboard to make the incinerator
a funhouse. We don't have money for the inside scare
but we get to see Skinny-Bones, the child-molesting child
come flying out of there, his blond head covered
his whole bloody face.

Sparrows scatter when you lean to hang clothes.
You say they sing for you. One winter morning one didn't
heed your warning tug.

Caught in the rope and pulley, he fell instead of flying.
You ran to revive him with breath and warm hands, bread
and melted snow. Your tears at his grave taught us grief.

Corn

Glide alongside as we cross the grassy hollow
where the highway ends, where cars whiz by
our feet bare, hands empty, towels in the wash
our suits on, stomachs bound for hot cement
pool-side where the whistle blows
and we jump in where you are nine and I am ten
where we teach ourselves to dive until at five
we cross back home to hear the clop and clatter
of the peddler's horse and wagon and the echo
in the alley of his chant where women with kids
too young to leave on upper-story porches
tie a basket to a rope and pay their money down
and reel up change and tomatoes and corn.

Nobody's Perfect Parents

Stay close, damp lamb's wool:
cling to the mouse-breasted color guard
who leads the Saint Patty's Day parade.
One more skinny girl tossing her baton
ahead of Shriners and Mummers
and somersaulting clowns. Marchers pray
for sun and balmy weather. Kids
hope mostly for balloons. But mothers
know kids choke on pieces of popped ones.
And they don't like cotton candy.
Or watching out of open windows.
Too many refugees in too many windows:
sick old vacant stares—nothing to do
but haunt the world with memories
kids learn about in school. And kids
on porches: Porky Wadman falls
four stories—and still our mothers cave.
Balloons lifting us off the ledge
whisking us up and away. And we're
gone longer than our building, which didn't
burn like so many others, but fell
to make room for the highway. When
the route was changed Grenier bought
the lot, built a stucco Atelier he christened
811, though it had been 810 Main
changing even to odd. You see it
on the sign where the highway ends.

Comeuppance

My brothers called me Cinder-Elephant.
I did their chores and never let them
forget it. A six-year-old dropping letters
in the mail, running out to Chappy's
for milk and bread. Down the front stairs
up the block to the mailbox, crossing
Jackson on the light—easy enough—though
I once mailed the dollar for the milk.
Coming back was hard and one time
awful. The hallway dim; the sun barely
got in; every landing looked the same
uncannily quiet—like everyone moved
while I was out. I could've come
back by the alley, I might've spared
myself, might've lingered in the yard
—but I wasn't allowed in the yard since
roughing up the boy upstairs. His
sister, dark and glowing, I asked to play
kick the can. I grabbed her by the arm
and spun her till she fell and got up
and ran, screaming in Spanish like it
was my fault. I settled on her brother
on his bright blood drying on my
knuckles. They were going back to
Puerto Rico: this my way of saying
goodbye. An afternoon too flush with
victory—I had to pay it back. Our
mothers were friends. I had to say I was
sorry. That was bad enough, but the
real payback came three days later as my
own careless brain, losing track, let me
climb an extra flight, the landing spotless
identical to mine: I bang on the door
of their vacant apartment, crying, "Mama
where are you? *Lama sabachthani?*"

Felicity Cast from the Garden with Swords

A wooden fence enclosed our porches
though it couldn't stop their sagging.
It saved a few daisies from being crushed
by cars—though it shaded them out
along with a tangle of milkweed and wild
plantain. A parking lot for tenants,
its unassuming familiarity the only stay
against its watchful glare. And as it
breathed out life we imbibed it: the gnats
and crickets, sparrows and flies.
This we did with thanksgiving on our lips
though it wasn't often pleasant. It was
almost always nighttime—a rain cloud
laden with comedy. We seldom saw
the situation clearly. Bats caught a glimpse
of squalid reality—we didn't often dwell
on the lives they might've led. Pigeons
on our stomachs: was it truly the end
of their being? A small intestinal star
could've shone for all the pain they provided.
Sometimes we wished we'd been gentler.
Our fathers we envied, but they gave
parts of themselves we never wanted.
The 5th of November brought a winter
blast as the yard expelled us. We'd have
gladly stayed another dozen years.

Capital Afternoon

I try Roy for the thousandth time
find him neck-ready for hanging
for teaching me a word
they caught me calling the kid next door
I thought some variant of "horror."

Then while I'm trying to watch
the men fill a van with
Claudine's family's furniture
he's in my face with a headless Barbie
squawking, "Kiss me, I'm titty"
his thumb stuck in cleavage.

For the last time it's goodbye Claudine.
In fifteen years I see her again
and don't ask if she remembers.
I'm starstruck by her friend.
They're learning to be stewardesses.
Other guys keep me from
being the center of attention.
At least Roy isn't here. He's on a plateau

with his cow tails swirling in the mist.
I remember taking him to the playground.
I got my sister Jane's rope
and Roy by the throat.

I'd kill him on the monkey bars
but that would be too public.
We go behind some bushes in a corner
where I hang him for a moment
from the chain-link crosspole.
I tug my end until his heels lift
his face turns red and I'm out of breath.

Next day, swinging Tarzan style
on the flagpole chain

jumping 1-2-3 O'Leary with Jane
and then Roy's heroin. His conviction.
The length of his sentence.

I don't know about lumping lust
with justice or the passion
or the proof. And the playground—
What can I tell you?
Traffic island willow bush is all.

Tom–Tom Milk Song

If hiding behind a Cheerios box was
breakfast, was dinner licking a fork
so no one would sit in your place?
The way our mother remembers her
brothers and sisters—a whitewash.
Like supper milk on the table since
four. Too lukewarm to wash down
cake, just viscid enough to bring up
the gorge. My sister complained
there were motes in her milk. She'd
eaten her cake, dropped crumbs in
her cup, thought she'd not finish
milk tainted like venial sin. Like the
blood of an only child if not for the
brother shining his eye-light, wishing
he could go unseen on nocturnal
prowls, smelling skin and bone like
no one more or less invisible than
Hermes, the worm-perfect pervert.

Sleep II, Day IV

So much for childhood. I had a zippered leatherette.
My sister didn't want it. It was large, impractical.
A slippery rind like a cheap new football. Every
way the perfect schoolbag. Painted-on piano keys
I scraped with a thumbnail: black and ivory snot to
flick across the aisle. The first family property I
could blithely destroy: the zipper tore from cramming
math and history. The music I would later use could
ride in the case with my instrument. My teacher
was a fireman on the overnight shift contentedly
wasting blazes when he could've fanned his flame
to beat the band. My other teacher said *imagine
kissing*—I didn't have a girl then. Did he think late
bloomers never learn guitar? I tell you I could've
been original—I could trace the face of each
beloved: noble gases swollen into planets, or any
swirling where neutrinos could've flown. Eyes
the thoughts we think, eat and drink what sunshine
provides then take us on a course a washed heel
never wanders. The mind one minute pushing into
blankness and the next finding light and full of song.

No Apology, No Clarity, the Waves Speak in Tongues

Secant
    summer
  where the planet casts latitudes
  cracks ice without melting

  my first guitar was a B52.
Oh, but that didn't make me cry.
    Sanded
  stratocast with glass frets

  it made a ripping sound
    like Tahitian saltgrass
remember? A wind stopper's subtlety
all girlfriendlike and pumice.

And you come cropping
  one spinnaker, one stack
  one ballast full of vinegar
  two sheets to the wind.

  You wouldn't catch me
  if I thought you wanted
  to stop mending nets
  to mourn injustice.

I'll give anchors to Asclepius
  before I sink my arches
in that half-hearted
  light. But you, brother

  conduct us Tiera del Fuego
  where the sun goes
  drowning in blue-floating vacuity
  and waters won't keep

their currents in.
  A tip of broken berg
with nothing hidden but its poverty

delivers us its body.

An ocean ravished
and we stand on the dunes
    packing caissons
    make shipping obsolete.

Six years without hope or birds.
    Trundled metal into trestles.
    Port authorities lace ankles
    and let us race the tide.

And this, what
    every good boy doesn't deserve:
    his mother in a way station
    losing cash and passport
    to the state-run

    poker video.
Meet me in the tunnel next door.
For cover you can hear
    untried youth

practice piano and drum.
    A long time ago she bought us
smoky blue-and-white-striped
      clam diggers
    gathered at the knee.

Hemp belts were tempting
but we preferred safe borders
imagining beach grass taller
than we were when we'd seen her
      drowning, treading

    her voice, sweet pride
though we'd never get there
when she rhapsodized how handsome
    how fun.

For Me Sign Painting Started as a Therapeutic Form

At fifteen I fell off the roof. Five months I spent
practically paralyzed. Narcoleptic clouds damped
my sense, and before I could manage a pencil
without tearing my insides, I'd stare at the shades
drawn for coziness and while away the twilight
filling the blanks with imaginary curve and depth
and color. Slowly I came upon in retrospect
what proved the likely subject. It helped me step
back and view pain objectively, covering posters
with metaphors for what I was feeling: fragments
of shibboleth, the big eating the little, sometimes
the little deceiving the big through dim warring
crowds, through broken glass in vacant lots, half
demolished buildings, tracts of milkweed, twisted
rusted metal, home of the mud wasp and scorpion.
It's been fifty years, and my head's still swelling
with dreams of people liking the stuff or, barring
that, running with a genius who one day in a pile
of signs connects for the first time to something
beyond him and claims me as his spiritual dad.
Even now I strain not to heal. Migraine and back-
ache the fuel my economy depends on. I nurse an
adder in my bosom. No light makes it in or out.
I won't lack for gifts to the world. Not if what
I give it mimics fashion. Stuffed pain and painted-
on spirit. That's not salesmanship. It's alchemy.

And Anxious for No One

I could chase parked cars
and never let them catch me.
I could navigate the head-
lands, coast through winter
wheat fields. I could live
at large at every point on
the trail as in the rooms at
either end. And the bricks
in corners of buildings
edging light in orange tile—
every mile an inching up
the welcome wall, rolling
toward the West Side Whale.
Patrons hefting giggling babies.
Kids with understanding
of clouds. I could handle
a breakdown. Pulling an axle
would relax me, but the
wrench keeps slipping
and the torch going dim.
And one hand wrapping
hankies around the other won't
stem the enmity ballooning
in my craw. Moods that
once held mismatched atoms
join a game shifting pot-
holes under shells. And I
haven't been breathing: the
pilings in my head: Lot's
wife warnings: waving blackened
flags in bloodless hands.

Out Here in the Fields

Okay, it's a parting of the veils:
the Department of Transport
    with its aura of harems and
holies, with its bustle
        its angel, its rank and its raise.

I was there to trace the way
    meanings change with
the symbols that express them.
Standing in a crossroads
where agents fall in love
where everybody comes to fall in love.

Sitting in a courtyard, knowing
    what to expect and how
to move on, or at least understand
when I can't sit or respond.

There was a girl whose lips and
scoliosis I couldn't be without

—but there I was, stumbling on
    steps her kisses had kicked me
clear of and landing in
    discretion, as if discretion
were a dog pile, as if Eros rids
    a body of its dross.
They could've shunned me
        or sent me into exile.
    I could've been questioned.
I could've used counseling.

    There may have been a line
in the sand, but I couldn't find it.
    Though on occasion
in my midden, never knowing

how I'll take it when the
    shakes hit, I can see
how understanding didn't block
    so much as limit
    my maneuvers, though some
had teeth, somehow brazen.
    So much revision.

    It's time I caught up
start acting my age
show how it might have been
if I'd slept with one or another
had one stair not led to a
fight that barely
started while another held me
responsible for freezing
    and flailing and

settling again in the dust.

    Some join the secret circus.
I, the severance brigade.
Others
as though nothing were wrong
understand understanding
    understand and move on.

Quaint Cake Row

The bookcase grew, material pouring in three nights out of five
with a streetlamp bearing witness, pallet pine from the dock
through the door of the walk-up where Guy must have done
keeping books in cardboard boxes. He could hardly take the smell;
it made him think of pine-scented sawdust dropped on grade-school
vomit, and it rung him like a Pavlov bell, but he slapped
his shelves together, though they'd rather split than take a nail
knowing they were good enough for paperback, thinking he could
get the pallets, thinking they were good enough for books
good enough for books and more than books, knowing he could
make a room take shape, then a wing or addition or an ell-shaped
apartment, then a Tudor colonial as seen on TV. Guy must have
tired of paying rent, he must have lost his low-tech ways
he must have struck it rich or borrowed money, since he bought
the land beneath him. He bought his neighbors' houses too. He had
to gut their apartments and concentrate their houses. He was tired
of their breaking in on one another. He had to make room
for the family and rebuild the Valley Arena. He was tired of the holes
they were making in walls. What he built with his slats hurled
splinters if looked at cross-eyed. What he built was self-referential
and splendid. His neighbors adored it. Others were bored.
They took umbrage at a slight provocation. His amphitheater stood
in their way. Their view had always been pastoral. They said
he lacked artistic integrity. Guy was too well versed in junk-art
ideology to salute their Jasper Johns. Confronted with the fear that
the place might collapse or catch fire, Guy fought, unrelenting.
When they said Herbert Hoover built a Bondo and adobe
cakewalk no different from his, he felt the rubric crumble
the baby fail to thrive. He strove to keep the shelving: it was
all he had after the ax fell. It could've been a bridge to starting
over. It could've been the lightning rod to ruin.

Old Colony, Little Canada

Because nature, in some of its putting together and
taking apart, suggests cures the body alone believes in
I head for Cathedral Oak, an hour and a half before
the end of my shift, soaking up the smells of an hour
before daylight. And the oak is alive, and I touch it
as we touched them as children in the park ages ago
where oaks were shaggy cousins of our elders
dwarfed by the Battleship and Germanium blocks
where mothers and fathers were maple, their mothers
and the Beaudrys, the Tanguays and Greenoughs
laughing on Sundays on shade-dappled benches, while
kids ran laps around tulips and boles whose knobby-
kneed roots could hardly slow us, but stopped us
with their curious skin, the black bark of unbowed
age. The Parks Department was planting saplings
my first birthday. My mother raised me to think
one was mine, given me in stewardship, my first share
of municipal identity, visible from a living room
window. A length of string held it steady to a stake.
It was small and hardly grew at all in our first 12 years.
When we hit our teens it filled out. By then we'd
moved to the Highlands and I only saw it on rare
occasions. Through the '70s and '80s the city changed
around it. Finally, the park itself was gone: trees
buildings, flower beds, benches. My maple looked mature
in its solitude. As for me, I've staked myself to slash-
burn economies, the kind that favor quick growth over
the slow persistence of trees. I wouldn't know the
child I was if he tapped me on the shoulder. A maple
on a traffic isle on a paved-over park: Who knows
what lasts? What I have is this live oak canopy, miles
uptown, all night crying me out to the wild.

A Type of Holiday

In spring, after the rain, after Chudacoff Falls and Lake
of the Clouds, where arrow-blazed cairns beckon on
to lofty slopes of sphagnum lawns, I invariably long
for the depot where I hop the whistle-stop south
anxious one moment, resigned the next, to the chance
that I'll miss the Symposium in the Wadsworth
Athenaeum on Apollonian Virtue in a Post-Apollonian
Age. There's more of habit than hope in my going.
I'd like to know if others in the audience feel the same
especially when the same young man stands and
confesses to the same subtle scopophilia, the same
predilection for high-stakes stimulation that I've come
to accept as my own historical precedent. He knows
what we want is a view from the top, so he climbs
the old balcony using the hidden stairs, and I feel it
coming—he wants to jump and be hanged, he wants to
be Grendel in need of a Beowulf; and that's when
I hit the ether, grab the mahogany banister and swing out
in the light of Canal, set a course for the Battleship
down streets that outline a Jesus fish, along South Suffolk
past Neisner's Five and Dime, past sporting goods
and strip joints lit for the evening's entertainment.
I hear a jackhammer's echo from work ended hours ago.
The pavement blabs with ethnic friction. Screams
and sirens echo along the vacant lot where the Bowl-
O-Drome was, past the factory outlet, in the clock tower
above city hall, on the path shaped like a whitefish
Rohan's and the flats where churches either burned
or blessed themselves dismantling. Eventually
I visit my father, as I do every June after the trip and
symposium, at the end of the fish walk. I barely
mention walk and symposium. When it comes to the trip
I go into detail. I try not to sound apologetic. I know
how much he liked the mountain, how much he'd

like to go if I didn't prefer the depot—if I didn't prefer
going alone like Amundsen, instead of with him like
Scott leading lieutenants. Our eyes glaze over
unresolved issues: tomorrow work; tonight a cartoon.
The dragon sick with fire cough, the sore throat and foul
mood—nothing more sordid than toasted tonsillitis.

No Free Energy

Without a law of conservation of body heat
it's hard to hide an interior whine. It
shows on the face while shaving, shows
on the lips and masks a massive sine wave.
It flattens the nose with an anvil.
The body ought to brook no deviation
in its conservation, no siege-state struggle or
infinitesimal strain. A guy should lope
with a lurch and still loaf on his perch.
Forty years of honest toddling ought to
lead somewhere. Once, on Mt. Moriah
snow sucked off a boot I hadn't properly
laced. Later, in a meat-locker freezer
no faces were familiar—the ones
I knew crossed the ridge while I lingered
on the slope—I had a premonition they'd been
stepped on. A's missing crampon
B's daring attempt. It's been ages since
I waved them on and struck out on my own.
And now, where we converge, beyond
the rainbow: the azimuth cathedral:
no better place to roll the asymptotic log.

Hurricane Coast

There were nights when a thin, well-toned dancer
could glance my way and stop a headache cold.
But most nights: no. Whole months flipped by where
nothing even tried to be exotic—and this was true
from Chestnut to Worthington, what we fondly
referred to as the Hurricane Coast. A scene so familiar
it bred quintuplets of contempt. It wrung from the
managers' pores, from the women tending bar, too old
to be dancers, from the middle-aged thug who might've
been the owner—he couldn't hide his smirk, strutting
from back room to break room. Was he tapping
the merchandise? I surely wasn't. But it was some-
thing after work. A short walk. No one getting
on your nerves. Everyone in his own separate fantasy.
Not like the singles bars. I'd see more fights in one
singles night than in a whole season of stews. Some-
times a look would excite me. I'd tip, talk, try
to be friendly. Then there was Gabriella. She said
I was cultured, but she was married, with a kid
at home and a boyfriend on the side. She wanted
me to help pour sugar into a rival dancer's gas tank.
I said no. My goal was to remain above the fray.
I'd nurse my beer, let others do the tipping. Did I care
what people thought? Once I found a bar in the middle
of a ball field, once in the loft of a barn. Girls on
break, same age as my daughter, playing Barbies
combing their hair, dangling their lives over graves.

Pin Drop with Orchestral Accompaniment

I grandfathered my father cruelly compared
to the way my daughter grandfathered me.
She had mercy: was thirty, married seven years.
I was fifty-two: I should've been role-ready.
My dad was forty-six when I was twenty-two
and begat my daughter. If he didn't like it
he didn't let on. He blessed me in rays
of shining water as we walked a mountain stream
his shadow on my daughter's and both of theirs
on mine, corresponding and everyone agreeing:
he could hold his anger in layers of silence
convinced that only patterns imposed with our
hands were worth our persistence. I could
write a book about water on the page
teasing then stretching the letters, imprinted
so firmly you'd have to soak it for weeks
to turn the letters blue, then blurry, the paper
turning to pulp before you'd render it illegible.
It was his trade, and he lost himself there.
Books did it for me: my heart bolstered by
newsprint on the hand, smudging cheeks
touching paper I'd give my shirt to keep clean.
The tattered edge of cellulose and the rose
the bridge café, the long afternoon's march
and the sun's taking leave. I was the first of six
—born when Dad's dad was fifty-nine.
They must have thought it was a new beginning
in the days of complementary coupling
ending in the webs that glisten in the mist.

North End Bridge

The night I left my keys in the door, John, whose own door, in plain
view of mine, was his favorite lookout post, swore he knew
nothing. He let me sweat, call a locksmith, deal with the manager.
Two days later, hemming and hawing, he informed me that he knew
who had my keys—and that he'd have to give this person two
packs of Marlboro to retrieve them.

I played along, drove him down Main and watched him enter
a tenement. To think I let him use my phone. I liked hearing him argue
in Greek with his mother: "Craxi pallaxi, Ma."

A few minutes later he emerged, spouting some vague story
about how difficult the errand had been—hoping I'd further reward
his efforts. I wasn't that big a fool.

He eventually lost the apartment
lived on the street out of a shopping cart, talking to himself.

Jim later became the neighbor. I'd help him unload his drums after gigs.
He talked me through a breakup and later helped me move.
I tried inviting him to my wedding but he never answered his phone.

For the few months between John's leaving and Jim's moving in
a guy in his mid twenties had the apartment. I didn't see him
much and don't remember his name. He stopped living there
right around the time someone leapt a car off the North End Bridge.

I was impressed. The bridge's concrete barrier had a wall-like aspect
that posed formidable challenges. The iron rail had been too easy
—half a dozen cars in the last twenty years had breached it.
After the last the railing was dismantled. Its parts lay end-to-end
in red September grass at the end of my street.

On Sundays my daughter and I play on the rails, pretending
our lives depend on I-beams we leap one to the next. Afraid of falling
into chasms, we laugh a breathy laugh and grab a saving hand.

Lives of the Curbstones

We proved we knew the way with our eyes closed
counting each step along Appleton, each theory
testing how best to negotiate the dark, keeping traffic
on our left while my sister and I cruised the curb
to its underworld. Caught in their concrete opacity
we'd say curbstones had all the appeal. If three
were shady, two were cool. If one knelt, we out-
prayed it. All that and the woman of the dunes.
I want to stop being jaded. I want to stop being sated
and forge a new covenant, leave the house of faucets
and the woman of the dunes, the sand Monday
morning, water Monday night, the woman secretly
plotting her leaving—she's no good at keeping secrets.
My sister asks me why I hide indecision in the
company of satyrs. I want to shake her and tell her
there's room for despair. I want to tell her that she
is my home—like the stones our curbs were cut from
—the ones I hope to return to. I can sleep in the car
if I have to. Sunday mornings tilt a corner of the mind
so still and so gray, thoughts glide like minnows
frictionless nothings kissing snowflakes, hints
of wing-beaten cloud topping tongue-burnt stars.

My Korea

I have to envy your sleep on the unstable mattress.
Mack trucks haul across my Philadelphia night.
I.V. drips from a tanker, a thin red line leading
back to Pyongyang, where your dad plays doctor
injecting GIs back from Japan with fun on their
conscience. He charges less than his Unit.
Inspections have him hiding needles in the pond.
You scratch, toss, moan with every exhalation.
I lick my palm and fret about your selling
used cars for your landlord. Like your father
courting disaster, like having a name like
Stufflebeam, nose buried in his smartbook.
Thank God boot camp doesn't last. One day
he's in Manayunk humping like a monkey
the next, like me, corporal in an elite corps
in the kitchen feeding mice. You give fair
warning: if they chew the electrical, kiss this
Christmas goodbye. I have to wonder if I'll
ever re-enlist. After your father—sleeping on
duty, abandoning his post for the heated cab
of a truck, then crying in his cell, clinging
to the chaplain, sobbing, "Don't let them
shoot me. My girl's knocked up—I'm friggin'
just a child."

More Women Selling Insurance

While searching in corners in four or five drawers
while looking for beneficiary forms
they arrive from the sophist's

the flowers with "Thanks"
on the card in Sor Juana's feminine back-slant.

And I am only grateful: so far as I know
she hasn't pinned
my series of detachments
to an aunt I fell for
and can't run far enough away from.

I was a link in a chain, a virus she got over
a cold she can't remember
a minor premise
of the cancer
that would take her
a desperation
that would do it soon enough.

With members of my family this can happen.

When sex no longer drives

we box it up and throw it
in a closet with unwanted sweaters.

Taking the lid off at two in the morning
still looking for forms
I spot a moving

shadow by the lamp, by the door I know
I closed. It's Uncle Butterfly, the widower monarch

his porcelain face in his round walnut frame
leaning toward a window

studied, puzzled
over cigarettes.
You could stand outside the diner

and set your watch by his numeral
the creeping minute, sweep-hand second

soft persistent tick.

Ashes from his wife's last rose
dust his wingtips.
I hold my hand out and he lights on my finger,
lifts me, fully, inches into the room.

Will

I swear I hardly hit her. Maybe punched her arms
or pulled her soft blond hair

—its smell like honeysuckle, warm running water,
her hair up under it, reaching with her neck,
flicking drops on her shoulders.

She'd lean her towel-turbaned head on my chest
and fall asleep on my lap.

Even with the shades drawn I could tell
it was snowing: paisley white and paisley gray.

She liked to pose in freshly drawn hieroglyphs,
a shadow caught mid-flight,
love that mattered less each day,

and spring that left me seeking assurance:

absence from the litany she enacts for new friends.
My name unspoken, particulars
forgotten.

No restraining order, no growing fond, no fiery
sword in her smoking mouth.

Meet My Commitments

Not a one of us held to account for Monday's missing reports.
I was certain I'd be called or at least written up.

I'd been busy with something my job description doesn't include:
I monitor rabbits who dig warrens on company grounds.

I'd been watching white scut drop behind Queen Anne's lace
and waiting for dusk for fireflies. And who would stop me?

The hub wants to scale us back and sell us off. It's courting
buyers and has no time for outposts in the hinterlands.

We're paid to be autonomous, some of us. Some of us
have the sense to curse the luck. Authorities return, frightened

of those above them. And yet, I am not a strict constructionist.
Machines and hands are interchangeably obstinate.

I request a vacation, citing holes I patched that are holding
and a dog-size solstice in the likeness of a cloud.

Making Friends for the World

If I lose my job and run out of benefits I'm in Mexico
where it's not so easy to freeze.
I'll scavenge what I can and steal my neighbors'
water. I'll get reckless and confuse it with
life to the full: jump bail, sharpen shank for
associates, fall beneath their pig-sticking
luminosity, the fear of the Lord in me.
I'll engage my last locust in a raid on the after-
life, blood threading every pore, but I won't
come north, like Leigh, to die in the cold.
She was thin in a thin blue coat, trembling in
the vestibule, grounded in New England
winter, yet well enough to flutter up and perch
in my apartment. Her name was Leigh.
"Pronounce it lay." She'd come home home-
less with a methadone Jones, an only child
in a city barely remembered. She said she
was dying of AIDS. That put an end to any
notion on my part. I made cocoa. It was 1988:
way too early for AZT. She sobbed, smiled
offered me a hit from her half pint. I declined.
Said I had to get to work. I didn't thank
her for her story. She thanked me instead.

American Elephant

My brothers and I on the sunny side, in the road
damping stubs, stamping out matches, more
frightened of mice than of men. My brothers and
I and the clean up. They're tall and don't offer.
"How could we?" they'd ask. "We're tall, but
you're older." Which may be why we never
left. We live within miles of the hospital and
the mother we were born in and out of. But the ties
that bind us are loose. Take these wandering
chestnuts, distantly related through Morganetta
a cousin from the Congo, first of her kind to
kick the amniotic cocktail and quit licking salt
in the all-night caves of Kitum. She founded
a colony in western New England—woke one
morning shackled to a concrete slab. Our
dreams may be meek, but we're better off than
she is, better than these poached and luckless
wonders. We're left with their remains. We
might help one another. Like Masons. Like the
Mafia. "Sure you're only two years older," the
middle one says, "but you're not much shorter."
Plus he has two daughters and custody. The
other, being taller, drags a ribcage to the yard
to file by weight, or maybe volume; we don't
ask, we only continue, slow with the task, our
cheeks full of secrets, our trunks thick as trees.

Then Publicans Raised Hells like White Elephants

What a breach: hearing a coworker
telling how her brother smacked his child.
The story, in harsh whispers, the detail
in the tone. There's no use pretending;
the narrator no one you'd pull for. Nor are
you (like the smoker beside her) the audience
intended—you're a standby without status
lost on the fringe: one too kind to be believed.
And it isn't good enough being good of
kind or kind of good. An off-room lavender
felt more than seen. The silence of a brother.
The idea that one can fall off a dock
of reconstructed newsreels that fill him
full of sweating from the nostril, like a beast
it's best to pretend to be in love with but
suspicious of, thrilled when it slips, giving
evidence that it might feel the same.

Springfield, February 14, 1989

I hear them coming from across the hall, as if the right kind of listening
could lift them over the building's musical digression
and lull the night skyward

part mirror   partition   walls too thin to stop their banging into sleep
where I'm caught in a Spiderman spin-off, panting, "Help! My brother
hangs by a thread, has two custodial daughters, and custody!"

Letting go is painful. The neighbor growls, panting.
The woman screams when she breaks his radio, calls him Charles the Slut
and cries till he slaps something into her. Like it's what he does.

But
ix-nay on the exposition. They might have been neglected as children.
They might have sprung full-grown from the pages of Popeye

though spinach can't save this unnamed Olive, immersed as she is
in the family amniotic. And though I've never heard the baby cry, I have
heard her, I've seen her push a carriage,

hiding her face in her hair, Charles walking behind her, his mind
in his beard—his thickly wired minister's black veil, nodding grim hellos.
None of which breaches the membrane that divides us

though rain swells the Connecticut, as if his violence
were liquid, as if the river scratched its black-and-blue ass to no end.

Hyperboreana

Taking shelter with an unmarried woman
whose namesake zealots murdered
on a third-century highway. Says she's
Egyptian but today's religion is no less lethal.
Some things you don't forget: how to
bend in a storm and slink like a tiger,
how to navigate drought from the floor of a cage.
Internal conflict is our latest threat.
Relaxation and impatience by turns take
possession of eyes and material objects.
Hands and their goals unite after mediated
separations. At the height of a solstice
bedroom walls weep. Read books
remain unshelved. I go days without
working. Hypatia cooked on the third
and I ate like a lord, enjoyed full
kitchen privileges, but I couldn't bear
the pressure of knowing where she stored
her pots and machines. Ice is not
the best insulation. Like French for
Indochina, no purchase by way of the past.
No heels half-moon the powdered
snow as if to flaunt our lack of hunger.

I've Been Giving More Thought to the Costume Jewelry Approach that Nature's Been Taking this Month

A light, calm snowfall
gives the streetlamp something to shine on.
"Shine on this," the snowflakes whisper.
The snowflakes drift, they catch the light.
The streetlamp is a manmade thing.
If you climb the pole
and put your ear to the bulb
you'll hear the buzz of electrons
telling how good it is to be steadfast.
You stand beneath the streetlamp
and tell it what to shine on.
"Shine on this, you manmade object
you steadfast object, you manmade thing."

What We Secretly Wished

Those soft pretty bodies with
play-pretty curves leaning between
lamppost and pillow wouldn't
see any boys or men but us.
Some push came shoving, leaving
winter in its wake, leaving a
name and a planet, no flag and
a mattress, leaving us wishing
for the hollow-eyed aunt, the
homecoming bash, the slaughter
of the fatted calf, the brother
whose wife can't stop dancing
at our wedding: she knows
this is nothing. We can have
our welcome-back and stipend.
We can have our wives and kids.
What we cannot have is our
fair share in the family concern.
It's our heart's desire, to get by,
see the kids through school.
What we have now: a strategy
for averting our gaze, though for
all we know we'll lose one another
buoyed by success, one shot
numbing for the last temptation
the once and fictive muse.

Ovidian Love Songs and Their Place in Radio History

Should the spineless backslide lose all trace of its negative heritage
where would we be?
Maybe finding detractors unable to pin us would inspire us to vanish
leaving only our tongues flapping with pride.
What we need is a song we can bend to. When we crack we mend
but we wouldn't even crack with the right kind of music. Every song falls
into one of two matched sets known as cornucopia and the void
all the while unveiling dream taxonomies of spirited
knaves whose aching hearts hold true case histories
"frauds so well conducted" only a fool would refuse to be moved.
Refusing doesn't work. Much like refusing to work. So here goes mine:
whose love is a wire, drawn through ever smaller dies, freeing
Daphne from the laurel, Jean D'Arc's heart from the heretic pyre.
Should your well run dry I will wed you back to water.

Of Every Glass Footbridge

Your nonsense eases elephants.
A lakeside tan that shines its weight in gold
and leaves pale patches in shadow.
A bruise
worn for effect with élan.

The trick—to jump and be taken
—oh, the wind
isn't needed; you can float in any room
find the single most weightless magic any
kiss can be given, any thirst

or draft of knotted strands.
Lips I'd cross on knees
if knees could bear the weight of
toads Egypt rained on Job.
Or the wrath unwinding in your mother
whose flood of love would sweep her
off the land.
Crumbling wall
her water was bound for:

where she found the brick she tried to warm.
Wind lifts, brushes our hair
cools her heart, the cool remains
of constellations.
It cools our laugh
blows the fairy tale to pieces
years wedged between our names.

Night to Quit Smoking

Winter's early sunset never was a problem.
Driving east out of daylight, aiding and abetting
the dark, proof that bodies could merge there
like accidents about to happen, where any
hill and any love might whisper promises in
silence, tag ends hanging out of either side.

Décolletage of deciduous hardwood, finial
carvings of conifer, stacks of firewood
light overtakes even as its source recedes
all green and radial gold. Silence a body could
wear on a pendant on a pond late winter in
a city in New Hampshire where mist blooms
in branches, a pulse beats in stars.

Nobler Shrewsbury

You weren't sultry, getting
undressed in the only dry room.
You might have been somber
leaf-showered, late-winged
kneeling under October rain.
Nothing should be added
to your silence
your last summer's cinders.
Mourning becomes you.
A mindless caress
might be better.
Let's touch tonight, let
me bear you, body-simple
to a tavern in town.
A change box, taking
dollars, spitting
dimes at dime-swallowing
slots there, let's let
a lot of French-speaking
singles sing something in Dutch
anything to remind me
of you, all
things refined. You
forgave the way I used
my looking poor to
ward off outstretched hands.
Once-loved songs go
begging to be caught
and forgiveness
hiding behind it
can't unslam the old
won't ring anything new.
Do you still have the key
to the Apple in Pocket?

What you said about
the lamb there was true.
What must have all smelled
burnt offering and
the end of an era:
neighbors warmed
by cold spring fire
the sky spitting gin
poured last Wednesday
in the Bistro on Main.

Vote with Your Aeroflot and Shoot Your Dame's Rocket

You never did intend to hide the
pounding in your temples
how horribly your head ached
as we gathered the garden's
October phlox.
Your anabolic argument
masked the fever
that was eating you.
If I'd known I wouldn't have
been meaning to ask
if you'd been meaning
all this hydraulic heating
piped into our veins.
At times it makes
survival hot at best.
Once we'd have been
major participants
our drums hung on
ancillary marchers
slowly timing our
pulse to the pull and
beat of the tide
bused to the common pier
without bending
heavy lifting or fear
of flagging in our own parade.
Okay, what happened:
We no longer want
what looked appetizing.
We use the language of the market
to rail against the running
of the early birds.
We sound cylindrical
rolled steel bells
instead of ancient hautbois.

One of us has to stop letting the other
make us plant-like
like TV's antacid spores
one tacit elbow
always on the verge
of wetting the moon.

Year of Bad Gardening

Salvia beds
mucked and wrapped for winter
with time, before snow
to steel for spring's trap

—which we have no way to avoid.
At least I won't
sneeze and fall in love.

Rain alleviates the sinus.
The baby smiles and frowns.
Moods pass like clouds

the drone faceless pilots use
to scud our afternoons.

Sodium salted Earth in
chlorine for protection.
Each liquid-filled
lady's slipper, light and ankylosis.

I mistrust rhododendron,
its way of growing where the bodies are.
The dog barked
with the same chuckling
cluck for days.

Night unfolds
accordion arpeggios.

Fire, a kitchen-witch
blooms
mid-May and
leaves all green all summer.
Sky versus
squirrel. Gripping bark
sniffing canopy.

Rattles in the wind like one of your
bird boxes. Your car
up to the waterline.
Your inventoried orchids.
Hepatica.
Bloodroot having
no prior record.
Shoots of indiscriminate
primrose rooted out with fleabane.

Fantasy knew
when love came, it'd go.
Its sylphs compete
with lovers.
They make everyone
uncomfortable.
They wouldn't matter
those weightless
waifs

if love didn't
complicate every afternoon.

Jays' feet tangled
in netting.
I'd rather not have blood
on my hands—I
forfeit blueberries.
Next door's willow
shades
the coreopsis.

Bad weather blossoms
everything blossoms
rose blossoms.
Campanula's second coming
rivals the rhododendron's
though the latter's partial

abortive
like rust.

Robin's nest
without a word
beyond the ledge
eggs abandoned
in wisteria
absent as the hummingbird
escorted from the porch
on the tines
of a rake.

Late September
rosebuds the frost
spared
a week later open.
If you bring them in
they die.

A birthday for the minister.
Songs, encomiums, slides.
The minister and how
she manages so slender.
The thought of love
rubbed raw.
In the mudroom
stumps of impatiens
leafless and waterlogged
despite the day's last rally
their saucers rank

their spirits sick.

While sunflower
bends its back
the potted rubber's lost.

No saucer large enough
to keep it off the carpet.

Rake until snow.
Twice under maple.
Oak and chestnut
cling to ratty staves.

Broken glass by the shed.
Dreading what might be under it.
The cancer rate
in neighborhood women.

Baby's tooth. His
mother, an interview.

I've eaten apples
so smutty I might have
chucked the lot.

Afternoon in Afterlife

And I know before waking each wave of tenderness
the baby gives access to, paths like
                         velvet on evening's adolescence
a town like Rising Sun limning the West.

And here a hearth in the glow of a restful interior.
                         And here a soft place for landing.

I cradle my cargo, my baby, so big in my arms
I can't see my wingtips. It's the same with taking off:

never anything solid to push away from
and still you glide. I leap from the rafters in the market
in mid-afternoon and business
                         is so brisk nobody notices
when I lean and let go.
It's their new specialty garners attention:

a thin bundle bound at one end
                         a morbid shock of human hair
coyly packaged for rapid sale
—more fetish than fashion, I might add, as one who
collects them.

I only wear a T-shirt, a pair of shorts ready to hand
in case someone tries to stop me.
                         One cop scratching parking tickets won't
and the shock dangling from his rearview
corroborates my confidence.
                         Like the day's final run

full of land-grab, full of fishing holes and couples
full of picnic ground and fairground
         hairless head of the cowpoke I've been dogging
all shank legs and big charisma.
         Small tin soldier from where I sit.

Everything I want I assimilate: every upbraid
every sigh, and heavy-lidded languish.
No qualms invoking pity to cadge tobacco, stroll
      my baby, break my will.

Beebalm by Way of Tansy

Last summer I stumbled into Olson's
poems like I kept getting hung up
on the tansy blooming on their hillsides.
And I found tansy-in-itself, later
about the same time, in Sturbridge Village
in a dense, formal garden where I lingered
with my daughter, noting leaf pattern
and color, enjoying the odors and the
markings like the ones on shrines dedicated
to the memory of Ophelia, like tansy
for remembrance, a wreath in Valhalla
as strong in life as ever in love and death.
I thought it was the best combination
since Frost swung on birches when
Maximus rained all Dogtown around us
and Francis scooped us with his flowers
small clouds, and his company of trees.
Late summer once again, a premature desire
for a daughter's independence. Two
sun-drenched Septembers drinking in
the bitter honey waftings. One day with-
out her, adrift on nether flotsam, and
one day with, like tansy in autumn whose
trim reliable button makes me long
for bergamot's cousin, that scarlet feather
duster, that bitter cup of herbal tea.

Arrangements for Economizing Worship

On holidays it's normal for the twinkling of a star to flick
icing on provisional cakes. To rev but not meander:
striking patterns at the airport that replicate in wheat fields
strings of Xmas lights spiraling up through branches
of spruce where their loops stretch like springs, the boughs
bent as though weighted with chinchilla roosts: that's
the strain maintained in well-toned tendons. Pluck one—
in no small way you pluck them all. I'm talking about
Electra's good night's sleep—her first in a year that started
with her brother killing Clytemnestra, though both are steeped
to the elbows in blood. But let's not get ahead of ourselves.
It's sadness more than evil now: Aunt Eurydice's funeral
lunch at a small spa in Cold Spring. A chill, cloudy April.
A fitful afternoon. I beg Orfeo to stop by the under-
world. I want to see her walk with the sky beneath her:
sweet Eurydice—attractive in ways I'll always remember.
She isn't coming back, though. Abuela Athena blames our
admiration: our turning out to witness stops the song.

Astrophage at 40, The Calm Before I Squander My Inheritance

At first I thought she must be hiding
or out wandering the neighborhood.
That wouldn't be that alarming
given the relative commercial calm
of the cosmopolitan
shoe store and rotisserie.
She never did leave the house though.
I'd catch her heading for the attic stairs.
There was nothing
she could play with or disappear into.
       No steamer trunk full of heirlooms.
Everything we put up there
was small, or too hard to play with.
I tore into walls and soffits
looking for the hideaway.
There wasn't one.
She would simply be there behind us
when the episode was over
as though she'd just stepped into the room.
Once I carried her to the top stair
where, with the sudden sensation of passing
through an ion chamber
with a strong magnetic pull
she vanished from my arms.
She was gone almost an hour.
We moved to where we didn't have an attic
and I got this much:
she'd been having fun:
games with imaginary playmates.
There were aspects I couldn't understand
somewhat occult elements
       that I couldn't
bring myself to trust.

Like a Sam's Club Mephistopheles
you could pick off the shelf
for home or office installation.
After all, she was only six.
When I conceded the impulse
to rechristen her Faustina
and lay the matter to rest
"Let her have her heyday"
was how my mother greeted me.
"Christ, don't you remember?
You were thirty-three
flirting with the mysteries."

Neutrino

Stained glass, you wanted, the color
of rubies and blood, for the window
we didn't want curtained. A desk for
saving canceled checks. And the fire
screen, that loose-hinged triptych
that trigger of a memory: the rooms
I never finished clearing out of
a few years, a few apartments ago.

So we go, and I spot Maddie's
rusted pickup double-parked across
the boulevard. I wonder what's
become of her. Her voice was soft
and somewhat sweet. I remember
being smitten; she knew how much
I liked her, but I haven't seen her
since she helped us move, and now
her last name eludes me.

So on through porch and hall: no
sign of the neighbors, and there
they are: the floor lamp, coasters
a few books on ethics, extension
cords, rubber cement—things we
accumulated while living abroad
furniture we bought together
the rocker you paid for, the seed
some sheet rock

loosely piled in the kitchen, as if
the place hadn't been occupied
since we left it. Someone
had been coming in to open and
shut windows, flip switches on

and off, knowing we'd be back
for the *Heloise and Abelard,* the
headboard we could use

for the kids. I can't help feeling
we're about to be accosted. We
can hardly expect to find what we
hid behind tan tassels under the
overstuffed chair. And yet it's
uncanny: how left alone we are
how unmolested and alive.

Who Got Your Red Riding Hood On?

In good faith, when you took the second call
I lowered the carrots so as not to

overcook them. But you were on the phone
so long they seemed about to simmer to a mash.

I swore I wouldn't let it happen.
—I'd turn the burners off and eat alone.

With or without me, sleeping or eating
hot, cold, lonely, alone

—it never seems to matter. You never
pay it any mind. Someday somebody

not so married to the mark will come along.
You think you'll blow through my funk

while I shuck live cohogs?
Keep your clients on the cutting edge?

See me scour pots and watch the news
while you sink your teeth in my paella?

The Cheese in Every Trap

All hours snow would melt while the warmth of our gaze
welcomed back brick and moss until night brought new layers
added inches, socking flagstones in for days. We could miss
a night's work, Em chewing wisps of hair, saying, "Everything
about us in time," wondering whether it were possible
to conceive in this weather. We ease back on calories
run in the road, Em wishing the prison were further from the igloo
so we wouldn't have to hear the feral boy lead a solitary
riot in his cell. But I like knowing what he's up to now that
the bars of his crib are more construction site than
containment field, full of baled wire and planks for building
in the snow. It's all part of an elaborate escape plan.
A melting fraught with reversals sends growth into leaf mold
and he thinks he might follow it under the crust.
A gossamer weave where the snow was, like moths' wings
a planet of runnels and worm trails, sinkholes and clouds that
torque of freedom and touch his tonsils into song.

Canto

If there was one dependable
aliquot in the dull hours
we were born to in a universe
pocked with plenitude it
was the music of the spheres.

The '80s were a mixed bag
caught between radios
tuned to different stations.
You were dead
and I didn't know. I kept
thinking I'd run into you
in Harvard Yard or
Holyoke Center. I'd have
grabbed you by the arm—
"What news on the Rialto?"
Had rap caught you unawares
half-morphed disco into
rhythms you could stomach
or would one look
have told me not to ask?

Music gave us tools to
improvise permissions
—any place we listened
sounded large. Rifts
we filled between houses
shrunk the continental
divide, turned shabby
trysts to bowers with songs
to bloat the ego, songs
we got high to
songs that got us high.

Those who spoke against you
at your hearing were
baffled by
your sad-sack hilarity.
You courted their approval.
It wasn't expulsion you
feared so much as
their banning you
from campus beer halls.

They said I was hesitant
when I said what a
friend you were. I hardly
saw you after that
—and after our final brush
with angel dust.

I had to slow down
to survive. Had to cultivate
patience, wait by the radio
a songbird fancier out
to catch a favorite tune.
But like nightingales in cages
their charms always fade.

I know small changes
precipitate disaster.
I could've tried to warn you
you were half in love
where I couldn't follow

and the best I can do is
keep grief from songs you
inhabit here and hereafter
in the sun and sublime.

Forty-Two and Through with School

Last night the sleep of a sandman's minion
   waiting for guns brought to church

for the first bingo to pay for covering the swastika
for downsizers eager to disarm the unarmed.
I awoke and checked the baby.

He'd been the life of the party.
He opened Leninger's *Biochemistry* for maybe 10 minutes
on Saturday. I told him to tell me if he needed help
but he only wanted leaving alone.

I could use my energy to sleep.
I could wait till I feel really awful
before I try to get things done.

Binding arbitration with my mother.
Caulking the bathtub with my wife.
We haven't been out since sitting on the piazza
with our tenants two tables away
and the baby so grown up.

One of my fears is that a program sweating
on a mouse pad
one night forecloses on my mortgage.
Not out to get me
—I see that from the start; but low performers
   should really be renting.

Somewhere I've a copy of the last Old Test
the last will, the wild country
where John the Baptist left his motorcycle.

     There's a fear of doing well
under the circumstances and a fear of failing
   when conditions improve.

I've been meaning to make a will
and a history of this headache.

I overcame my hatred of doctors
—it was only when I was told I had nearly
        taken my life

    that I put my papers in order.
I never had the slightest wish but to leave

my headache its very own mineshaft.

My freewheeling speech I leave dry and undelivered.
It's been the staff of life
—please handle with care.

My excuse I leave six flags of Jupiter
the one-sided rose

the left of Kilimanjaro.
The north face I leave my broken mouth
to which I leave commodities.
My family I leave illuminations.
    I want to make it as light as teeth that

I suppose will grow when I've gone.

They'll play the first tune you hear
coming out of the bathroom:
    the piano Uncle Phineas gave us.

I try holding the paycheck dry
but with the tub overrunning the last few days
it's hard not to take your money.

The Holyoke Diaries

With Mary safely married to her
Doctor, her 18th-century Holyoke heir, what remains in
Salem after the witch hunt but to take my stand

in the page of her diary

kept during the birth of a nation
long before my shadow crept out of the river park
her father-in-law graced with his name.

She who at the onset of war
whose necessity her neighbors
found difficult to grasp
had reason to wish away
whose outcome no one could know
would be called Independence
would move her household to Nantucket.

Doctor's orders. Wanting children
out of harm's way.
Neither saying which side they feared most
—they might have been Tory for all

that his diary ends before the war.
The issues must have been confusing.
Every town celebrating Stamp Act repeal
as much from hope the war
might be averted
as that the Colonies could win.

Not many stood to profit.
War, when it came, left her weary
persevering, reticent. Not silent.

Buried neighbors, family, friends
between this and the French and Indian

buried her eldest daughter
in a lull between smallpox and quinsy
consumption and quarantine. An earthquake
shook the country that summer
left all the windows and much china
in pieces. Left us drought, which
longer prayer meetings would help

see us through.
With dances, chills, tea and shoes.
More sickbed death than casualties of the field.
Wines by the case-lot from Italy.

Beer the beverage of preference
as told on banners single-engine
crop dusters flew above the beach.

With Mary gone, almost no one in Holyoke
would care who the town was named for.
By the time I came of age
that kind of plane was so outdated
not even my parents, a generation with grandchildren
could remember.

And yet things in the sky today
are so boldly of their time

they dazzle the best of us.

Strange steps paved the way:
star-shaped foil that bobbed and wafted
through 90-degree turns
of red, white and blue

demanding allegiance.

Soap bubbles! Trifles!
What we have now isn't meant
to supplement radio or TV.

Nobody with discretionary income
watches or listens.
The colorful productions
meant to ensure big numbers
preempted by typhoid and cholera

pleas from the edge of a war
on a scale Mary might have imagined
if she thought at all of Hell.

We look to the sky for comfort now
for birds and boughs

for cloud-like holographic billows
Madison Avenue learned to
project on big-city haze
just beneath and slightly behind
small-town cumuli.
When the weather is right
they drive them in and out
like so many domesticated moons.

On the day
the new antibacterial gel was unveiled
images drifted out of the northwest
in the same direction as
the weather, but slower, so that
it seemed already likely
while they were still 15 miles off
their trajectory
would keep them across the river
and over the West Side rather than downtown
which was fine with me.

The prospect of having
a toothpaste missile directly overhead
made me want to spit.

I hiked the trail from Central Hive
to the river. The restaurant
I hoped to lunch at was closed.

Maybe it had to do with not having eaten
and finding so many cooks put out
by high costs.

Maybe I connected the tubes overhead
with what Em said

about tartar control
being the root of increased sensitivity
cured by
switching to the anesthetic brand

in a ploy like Big Tobacco's
soaking up
stock in stain removal.

And a woman in the street whose grandchildren
kept getting close to the edge:
I thought for sure
they were going down the embankment.

The rush-hour press closed in.

Everybody was looking up from what I could tell
though I couldn't speak for the drivers
but I can't imagine they weren't the least tempted
to lift their gaze from
the bumpers in front of them.

And the woman with the grandchildren
wasn't as careful to keep them
away from the curb as I would have wanted
and I thought I would either tell her off
or turn her over to the cops.

There on the corner
falling on a parking lot
with only a little noise above the traffic
the latticework remains of one of those cheap
kite-like floats businesses use
who can't afford better.

I needed vacation.

That wasn't to come for a while.
Instead I did what I did in those days.

The city hadn't yet slapped usage meters
on information appliances

and I was addicted to news.
Now any just grates:
snails' traces of phosgene and refugee
movement too repetitive to listen to
but burned for back then
because illicit and unpaid for

and so like a drug for the thrill
the dailiness, hours on end, at home.

The space inside a small apartment deepens
with all that happens over time.
A well at the center of
which the life around us pours.

If a building stands
for two, three hundred years
it scintillates with history.
A neighborhood commons.
Its tragedy and fallacy.
Salem, for too many years
condemning single women.

At night my work
consisted of little more than
something to read, something to eat
an empty office, watching paper
stack behind a printer.

I used to have a partner. We'd sit
with our feet up and
it was only after the invention
of something I knew nothing about
that I got the day job and learned
to love the daylong hubbub
that leaves me drained and little interested
in iteration after iteration.

By then I'd married Em.
By some freak sowing of prescience
last October her dentist
found a tumor on her jaw.

We'd had our vacation.
Twenty rooms at a fingertip on
Pleasant Bay. Em's parents
brothers and sisters, nieces and nephews
along the hall; 20 rooms
water on three sides, an island
sandcliff across the channel

with a structure, a parallelogram
that looked familiar.

The map said Sipson Island.
A note tacked beneath the legend warned
of violent currents through the Narrows
with the tides.

I didn't think it could be that tricky.
I could throw a stone across
where it was over my head.

I imagined a path
as the crow flies, over land and sea
to the outer margin
a beach I could bodysurf.
A short walk to the far end of Sipson
another swim, a long wade.

One of the brothers and I swam to
where the steel-framed parallelogram
appeared less familiar.

The following day, introduced to Mary

I didn't ask how the diaries came here.
The owners were not Holyokes.
Family pictures on the walls
shelves of books in every room.
In-laws spoke their initial reluctance to rent
what to all appearance was a private residence
while I was unable to tell whether the
copy of the diaries

like the pictures on the wall
spoke of a connection between families
or cool historical curiosity.

Mary never mentions Pleasant Bay
having spent the better part of the war
on Nantucket. Brief news
concerning the children.
Nothing of relations with the husband
she unfailingly calls "the Doctor."
She isn't confessional.
Two or three entries per month
none longer than a line and a half.
A catalog of daily bread.
Firkins of butter.
More funerals than weddings.

Then out of nowhere an essay
on something "vulgarly" called a "cold"
knocking everyone around her for loops.
Later her own illness
documented briefly, without
embellishment or insistence.

Breaking out bacon.
Burning chimneys in spring.
Trips to Hadley and Cold Spring
which later became Belchertown
—temptingly close to Holyoke.

I didn't read to the end.
That day the wind picked up
scouring beach and hill.

The tide began to rise.
Where yesterday the bay had been glassy
seas made swimming impossible.
Em became confused
when I tried to explain
that Mary hadn't let her diary
register passion.

"Except for that bit
about the common cold."

In the distance above Nauset
a Piper Cherokee hauled a message
flapping wildly, too far off to read.

A warning
for those of us without radio and TV?
The notion of a weather advisory never occurred;
we could see all the weather
we cared to.

When the breakers began climbing
everyone was reassured
against a background of singing and
piano lessons for the young.
But I knew when the water began lapping at the porch
after having steadily inched its way
and nearly engulfing the house
I knew if we didn't leave soon
we'd wind up trapped.

I tried finding something on the radio.
I don't say I wasn't frightened.

Early detection, radio, dope
make cancer fearful, inconvenient
like this wave
after surgery, looking for somewhere to recover
and every hotel packed.

Interlocutor with Balloon

On the way to the young child's party a dog runs out and there's no time to stop and you hit it. It slides thirty feet on salted snowy road while spinning on its side. I check the ditch. You knock at the neighbor's. But it's gone. Gone to die in snow without words. Nestled under sheets and sheets in light and heavy beds. Reunited with its mate its mother litter siblings death the best a dog can hope expect. Blood-red winter letting bankers sweep the walks and fill the sheds with coal. Dead as your grieving the death of a dog giving nothing but love not having any other way to hurt you and she ran in front of a car—not a death she freely chose but hearts hold only so much grief. You could be ten and afraid of death again if your luck ran out. Let's go to the party. I'll cut loose a balloon. You tell me where you want it tethered. What you want it tied to. I'll hitch it to the moon and reach you down a fountain full of swallows.

Slowpoke as Portrait of the Fourth Degree

As dawn is my custom, I shall not balk.
As the access of color unfolds in its abscess the face
I once was wont to kiss on account of its never never lasting

I will meet its demand on the means of production
and resist the urge to call it capacity.
Its artwork is late
and I work 'round the clock to its deadline.

The dawn is where I shop for custom finery.
A give-and-take less
preconscious than symbiotic, something
akin to the mercenary romance one mistakes
for love or barter.

The body is a shop I'll not be confused with
though it takes me to landings where
music falls like summer rain.

The family are everyday shoppers
I shall avail myself of at least some few hours.
For they are most like the dawn.

Cut oranges are my custom. Served on their sides
navels trussed with pins.

      Shaking out earth's pleats.
Smoothing out its kingdoms.
I walk the folds and cubicles, a bouncer to shield me lest I flinch.
Stars line up like sheep.

The glissando of melted glassworks.
Apple Betties: *Je suis, tu es*

Insurance: the idea: pitching in
in time of need.

End of Poem: Yep, Right, Yeah

Let's weigh obligations: the blossoming canola
the smell of the river, the mortgage and I don't
know how we'll pay for the oil. So to hell. It's
colder than any spring our bodies wrapped their
fat in. So cold, schools close. The kids would
rather toss straw than mend walls. We'll keep
them home if we have to. Teach them to polish
icons and do their stoichiometry. There's a fuse
that sputters in the sweat lodge. Loopholes with
peepers and butterfly nests building in. As it is
like spaniels and their arias a few months on the
plains, whatever else we do, we'll pay for this
this house without a cellar, no attic and no well.

Acknowledgments

2River View: "Afternoon in Afterlife"

88: "Hyperboreana," "Ovidian Love Songs and Their Place in Radio History"

Alternative Reel: "Old Colony, Little Canada"

Argestes: "For Me Sign Painting Started as a Therapeutic Form," "Out Here in the Fields," "Year of Bad Gardening," "Neutrino"

Citizens for Decent Literature: "Making Friends for the World"

The Comstock Review: "End of Poem: Yep, Right, Yeah"

Electric Windmill: "Then Publicans Raised Hells like White Elephants"

Front Porch Journal: "Tom-Tom Milk Song"

FutureCycle: "Forty-Two and Through with School"

Gloom Cupboard: "Lives of the Curbstones"

Juked: "Will," "American Elephant," "Arrangements for Economizing Worship"

The Lucid Stone: "Nobler Shrewsbury"

Main Channel Voices: "Interlocutor with Balloon"

The Massachusetts Review: "Astrophage at 40, The Calm Before I Squander My Inheritance"

The Naugatuck River Review: "Comeuppance"

The Pedestal: "Sleep II, Day IV"

Poetry East: "Who Got Your Red Riding Hood On?"

Prick of the Spindle: "And Anxious for No One"

Samizdada: "Meet My Commitments"

Silkworm: "Springfield, February 14, 1989," "Of Every Glass Footbridge"

The Sonora Review: "No Apology, No Clarity, the Waves Speak in Tongues," "Vote with Your Aeroflot and Shoot Your Dame's Rocket"

The Temple: "I've Been Giving More Thought to the Costume Jewelry Approach that Nature's Been Taking this Month," "The Holyoke Diaries," "Slowpoke as Portrait of the Fourth Degree"

Third Wednesday: "Beebalm by Way of Tansy"

Thunder Sandwich: "My Korea"

About FutureCycle Press

FutureCycle Press is dedicated to publishing lasting English-language poetry books, chapbooks, and anthologies in both print-on-demand and ebook formats. Founded in 2007 by long-time independent editor/publishers and partners Diane Kistner and Robert S. King, the press incorporated as a nonprofit in 2012. A number of our editors are distinguished poets and writers in their own right, and we have been actively involved in the small press movement going back to the early seventies.

The FutureCycle Poetry Book Prize and honorarium is awarded annually for the best full-length volume of poetry we publish in a calendar year. Introduced in 2013, our Good Works projects are devoted to issues of universal significance, with all proceeds donated to a related worthy cause. Our Selected Poems series highlights contemporary poets with a substantial body of work to their credit.

We are dedicated to giving all of the authors we publish the care their work deserves, making our catalog of titles the most diverse and distinguished it can be, and paying forward any earnings to fund more great books.

We've learned a few things about independent publishing over the years. We've also evolved a unique, resilient publishing model that allows us to focus mainly on vetting and preserving for posterity the most books of exceptional quality without becoming overwhelmed with bookkeeping and mailing, fundraising activities, or taxing editorial and production "bubbles." To find out more about what we are doing, come see us at www.futurecycle.org.

The FutureCycle Poetry Book Prize

All full-length volumes of poetry published by FutureCycle Press in a given calendar year are considered for the annual FutureCycle Poetry Book Prize. This allows us to consider each submission on its own merits, outside of the context of a contest. Too, the judges see the finished book, which will have benefitted from the beautiful book design and strong editorial gloss we are famous for.

The book ranked the best in judging is announced as the prize-winner in the subsequent year. There is no fixed monetary award; instead, the winning poet receives an honorarium of 20% of the total net royalties from all poetry books and chapbooks the press sold online in the year the winning book was published. The winner is also accorded the honor of being on the panel of judges for the next year's competition.